# Inside the Introverted Mind

## Understanding the Mysteries of Introverts

**TERRY M. WALKER**

# Table of Contents

# Chapter 1

## <u>DEFINING INTROVERTS</u>

Introverts are those who tend to feel more comfortable and rejuvenated in alone or low-stimulation environments. They frequently prefer spending time alone or with a small group of close friends, and they may feel exhausted or overwhelmed at big social occasions.

Introverts are frequently contemplative and may seek alone time to refuel and analyse their ideas and feelings. It's crucial to underline that being introverted is a natural personality feature and not a bad quality.

There's a notion that introverted folks are someone who is afraid or quiet and wants to be alone.

While that may be true for certain introverts, it doesn't automatically indicate all introverted folks are the same. Some individuals are more introverted than others, others lie right in the centre of the spectrum.

To put it simply, introverts typically have a few extroverted tendencies mixed in with their introverted ones, and vice versa.

## TYPES

Studies questioned the assumption that introversion is a blanket word, instead, dividing it into four various sorts that affect individuals differently; social introverts, thinking introverts, anxious introverts, and restrained introverts. What divides one from the other?

### Social Introverts

This sort of person isn't fundamentally shy, yet they appreciate alone time or simple social contacts. Social introverts appreciate intimate gatherings and tranquil places over crowds. They tend to enjoy individual meetings over enormous parties, or one-on-one coffee catch-ups rather than brunches with a large group.

## **Thinking Introverts**

Often labelled daydreamers, thinking introverts spend a great amount of their time in their thoughts and tend to have creative imaginations.

They like hypothesising, generating, ideating, and narrating to the degree that it fills most of their brain space, thereby de-prioritizing other people as an inadvertent effect. Because of their strong introspective trait, they could come out as distant while they're simply studying the scenario and tend to be mistaken as being inactive as they are not fast to respond. Thinking introverts replenish themselves by employing time to self-reflect and explore their thoughts internally.

## **<u>Anxious Introverts</u>**

Anxious introverts prefer alone time because they frequently feel uncomfortable or embarrassed among others. They could feel extremely nervous in social situations and even when alone. Reserved is one way to identify neurotic introverts.

They will most likely avoid persons and locations that increase their anxiousness. While it could come out as avoidant or disagreeable, it's all merely their protective defence system operating. It doesn't mean they don't enjoy company, but they are highly cognizant of their comfort zones and don't want their limitations and bubbles to be crossed.

## **Restrained Introverts**

These introverts contemplate before they act, they aren't inclined to pick on a whim, making them generally demand extra time to take action.

A restrained introvert just doesn't show their cards immediately since it is often highly guarded at first. This makes people realistic and grounded in their attitude to life. But once you get to know them, they are willing to play with open hands. They also like dependable employment and can disengage from their emotions with ease.

Your introverted 'level' may alter over time, and in diverse contexts too. No matter what archetype you identify with most, realise that being an introvert holds many muted qualities when it comes to truly interacting with others, whether it is with your ideas, your sensitivity, or your well-polished ability to put up a party.

# STEREOTYPES

Introversion is not that easy for a layperson to grasp. Me being an introvert myself, it took me a lot of time to recognize and respect my personality type.

But now, let's dig deep into the complexities of introversion and question some misconceptions!

## Stereotype #1: Introverts are timid folks

This is likely one of the most misinterpreted contrasts when discussing introversion: shyness vs. introversion. But there is a major difference between the two.

Shyness is a predisposition of being fearful in a social environment, typically haunted/afraid of judgement and/or criticism. This leads to discomfort and worry for the individual.

Introversion is a significantly more intentional drive to stay passive in an engagement. It's a source of recharging and gaining energy via momentary silence/inaction.

Also, introverts are often highly attentive persons. And to witness other people and events, you sometimes have to silence your tongue.

Shy folks may be introverts. But not all introverts are shy: this is what's crucial to recognize.

## Stereotype #2: Introverts are obedient and cannot be effective leaders/speakers

Now, this is a little disrespectful folks! Just because a lot of introverts don't boast or oversell themselves, doesn't suggest that they concede or are not skilled enough.

We simply don't want to get in your face and shout about how amazing we are. We do it, like it, and feel secure, inside.

Note: I don't encourage, support, or oppose any action, opinion, or belief of any of the above-mentioned persons. Please concentrate on the point.

Please stop considering stillness or ignorance as a sign of weakness or ineptitude (I know a lot of you do; you are probably mistaken, my friends).

### <u>Stereotype #3: Introverts are anti-social; they don't enjoy being with people</u>

Again, not true. And this is absolutely illogical from a biological standpoint.

Every person has to socialise. It's only that the degree and mode of socialisation might change.

This is precisely the case with introverts. How we socialise and how much we socialise could considerably vary from extroverts' techniques of accomplishing things.

A lot of introverts take their time to find the perfect person to connect with. We could be a little more patient and choosier.

Quality above quantity is our credo. A few amazing friends are significantly better than a lot of acquaintances, in our lexicon.

## **Stereotype #4: Introverts are rude, dull, and strange**

I have to recognize that this is something that the other parties can't be accountable for.

It is tough to occasionally grasp and digest our manner of doing things. Plus, there can be a gap in communication from our side, which makes the matter even more complicated.

But believe me, we are not rude (usually). We may not be that eager to express and emote every time, which comes out as harsh or rude.

Also, introverts may be one of the most interesting folks in the room (the case for introverts being dull). We have the weapon of mystery; and believe me, nothing is more exciting than that! Just make some effort to grow close to us, and you won't feel bored ever again.

Speaking about weirdness, first of all, there are a lot of meanings and definitions for the phrase. But let's simply accept strangeness as conduct which is not very often. That could be true for us, I won't lie.

But what's wrong with that? I believe it's terrific to be eccentric; it's great to be unusual.

## **Stereotype #5: Introverts are not confident**

This one makes me giggle at times. I'll tell you why.

I have a theory that introverts may be more confident than a lot of people who are normally chirping and talkative.

So, here it goes:

When you are consistently expressing yourself in public, you are strengthening your possibility to come out as more appealing and interesting. Simply because you are performing it more often, which enhances the probability of achievement, normally.

This makes you more likely to acquire admiration and external affirmation. And external validation is an extraordinarily strong drug to boost confidence swiftly.

For example: If I am at a party and get a complement for my attractiveness, charisma, etc. I am likely to feel safe after that (for the time of that occurrence at least, unless there is some negative externality).

That's how outward affirmation makes you feel.

But for introverts, that probability is substantially reduced compared to the first group, as we are not continuously seeking to capture attention and express it aggressively.

I am not here to propagate that introverts are superior to extroverts or vice-versa. That's a ludicrous analogy, in my perspective. They both exist. They both are significant. They both are vital.

I genuinely hope that after reading this book, you understand introversion and introverts better than before. And will probably cease annoying them by asking unsound inquiries.

# Chapter 2

## <u>INTROVERTS VERSUS EXTROVERTS</u>

Introversion and extroversion are key aspects of personality that represent opposing ends of a continuum.

These qualities determine how people react to social circumstances, assimilate information, and restore their vitality.

Understanding the breadth of introversion and extroversion may help us appreciate the variety of human nature and give insight into the varied ways individuals view the world.

### <u>The Spectrum of Introversion and Extroversion</u>

Introversion and extroversion exist on a continuum, with most individuals falling somewhere along this range. At one end, we have severe introverts, who tend to be more quiet, thoughtful, and prone to solitary pastimes.

At the opposite end, we find extreme extroverts, who thrive in social surroundings, are sociable, and gain energy from interactions with others. In the centre, we have ambiverts, who display a combination of introverted and extroverted characteristics, modifying their behaviour according to the scenario.

### Characteristics of Introverts

Introverts are typically identified by their need for isolation, preference for one-on-one or small group interactions, and contemplative temperament.

They tend to feel more comfortable in calmer environments and may get overwhelmed or weary by excessive social stimuli. Introverts usually study information carefully and may hesitate before speaking, making them exceptional listeners and introspective thinkers.

## **Characteristics of Extroverts**

Extroverts, on the other hand, are recognized for their warmth, enthusiasm, and excitement in social contexts. They prefer being among others and flourish in group environments.

Extroverts tend to be more externally expressive, prefer taking chances and are generally viewed as powerful and outgoing. They may process knowledge by talking things through and tend to think as they speak.

## **Biological and Genetic Basis**

Research demonstrates that introversion and extroversion have a biological and genetic underpinning. Studies have revealed particular brain regions and substances that may be related with these attributes.

For instance, introverts may exhibit higher activity in the prefrontal cortex, engaged in decision-making and planning, whereas extroverts may show more activity in brain regions connected to reward processing.

### **Environmental Influences**

While DNA plays a factor, external conditions can impact an individual's personality. Cultural customs, upbringing, and life circumstances could affect whether someone develops more introverted or extroverted inclinations.

For example, an introverted kid raised in an extroverted environment may learn to adapt to social surroundings, blurring the lines between their intrinsic nature and learned actions.

# The Power of Ambiversion

Ambiverts have a unique combination of introverted and extroverted qualities, enabling them to flexibly adjust their behaviour depending on the context.

They may prefer interacting with others but also cherish times of isolation for self-reflection and recharging. Ambiverts demonstrate a flexibility that allows them to interact with numerous personality types and prosper in varied environments.

## Understanding the Needs of Introverts and Extroverts

Recognizing the varied characteristics of introverts and extroverts is crucial for supporting well-being and developing inclusive settings.

Introverts may require time alone to recoup after social engagements, whereas extroverts may need many chances for social engagement to feel revitalised and joyful.

## Embracing Diversity

The range of introversion and extroversion emphasises the great variation of human personalities. No personality type is essentially superior to the other, and each adds specific talents and views to particular circumstances.

## Introversion and Extroversion in Relationships

Introversion and extroversion may play a crucial role in defining interpersonal interactions. It is fairly rare for folks with opposite personality attributes to develop long friendships, complement each other's strengths, and balance out each other's flaws.

Introverts might deliver a soothing impact and a listening ear, whilst extroverts may inject energy and passion into social situations.

However, complications could occur when the various demands for social engagement and alone time are not properly acknowledged or handled. Effective communication and compromise are important to developing healthy and successful partnerships between introverts and extroverts.

## **Workplace Implications**

The link between introversion and extroversion in the workplace may affect team dynamics, communication styles, and job satisfaction.

Introverts may prosper in duties that need thorough research, concentrated effort, and attention to detail, whereas extroverts may thrive in positions that include networking, team cooperation, and public speaking.

Recognizing and recognizing the contributions of both introverts and extroverts in the workplace fosters a more inclusive and productive climate.

## The Evolution of Introversion and Extroversion

As groups and lifestyles grow, the perception and acceptability of introversion and extroversion also shift. Historically, extroverted traits have been more appreciated and rewarded, but introverted skills were typically misconstrued or discounted.

In recent years, there has been a greater recognition and appreciation of the qualities and distinct ideas that both personality types give to diverse contexts.

### Embracing Personal Growth

Understanding where one lies on the introversion-extraversion continuum may be a powerful tool for personal advancement. For introverts, embracing their urge for isolation and self-reflection may lead to greater self-awareness and creativity.

For extroverts, appreciating the necessity of introspection and self-care may boost their emotional well-being and promote deeper interactions with others. Embracing and fostering traits at the other end of the spectrum helps extend one's social flexibility and emotional intelligence.

## Addressing Introvert and Extrovert Bias

Despite greater understanding, prejudice and misconceptions regarding introversion and extroversion continue in society. Introverts may be misunderstood as being distant or apathetic, whilst extroverts could be perceived as attention-seeking or hasty.

Overcoming these preconceptions includes building empathy and learning that personality features are not inflexible stereotypes but malleable components of identity.

## Promoting Inclusivity

Creating inclusive settings that match the requirements of both introverts and extroverts is crucial for building a feeling of belonging and encouraging everyone to share their unique strengths. This means giving possibilities for meaningful cooperation, allowing quiet locations for introspection, and acknowledging diverse communication modalities.

## Embracing Your Authentic Self

Ultimately, the introversion-extroversion spectrum empowers people to accept their actual selves. Rather than complying with conventional standards, it encourages individuals to identify their natural inclinations while understanding the demand of adaptability in adjusting to different circumstances.

The range of introversion and extroversion illustrates the variety and diversity of human nature. Both introverts and extroverts give significant features to society, and learning and embracing these distinctions may lead to more harmonious relationships, inclusive settings, and personal advancement.

## THE SCIENCE BEHIND INTROVERSION

Introversion is a significant characteristic of human nature that has attracted academics and psychologists for decades.

While introverts and extroverts exhibit different behavioural tendencies and responses to social situations, understanding the science behind introversion goes beyond mere categorization and delves into the biological, neurological, and genetic underpinnings that shape an individual's inclination toward introverted traits.

This portion addresses the present scientific information regarding introversion, bringing insight into the delicate interaction of nature and nurture in shaping an introvert's character.

## Genetic Basis of Introversion

Numerous studies suggest that inheritance has a considerable influence in determining an individual's personality characteristics, including introversion.

Twin and family studies have revealed that introversion has a hereditary component, meaning that a percentage of the diversity in introverted dispositions may be connected to hereditary reasons.

Researchers have uncovered specific genes related with personality characteristics, such as dopamine and serotonin receptor genes, that may contribute to introversion.

## **Neurological Differences**

Neurological research has revealed fascinating insights into how the brains of introverts and extroverts absorb information differently. Functional magnetic resonance imaging (fMRI) studies have revealed that introverts tend to have more activity in brain areas involved with introspection, internal thoughts, and self-awareness, such as the prefrontal cortex.

On the other hand, extroverts tend to display higher activity in areas associated with external stimuli and rewards, such as the amygdala and nucleus accumbens.

## Brain Reactivity to Stimuli

One of the most fundamental distinctions between introverts and extroverts resides in their reactivity to external stimuli. Introverts tend to be more sensitive to external stimuli, and their brains may get easily overwhelmed by excessive sensory input.

This heightened sensitivity may explain why introverts may select calmer circumstances and less external input to prevent feeling overstimulated or weary.

## Cortical Arousal and Alertness

Introverts may demonstrate a stronger baseline of brain arousal compared to extroverts. This means that introverts tend to be more attentive and responsive to interior ideas and experiences. In contrast, extroverts may have a lower baseline of cerebral arousal, preferring external signals to boost their attentiveness and participation.

## **<u>Information Processing</u>**

Introverts and extroverts also vary in their information-processing techniques. Introverts tend to digest information more slowly, engaging in reflection and contemplation before reacting. Extroverts, on the other hand, may process information more externally, thinking out loud and seeking input from others.

## **<u>Brain Chemistry and Neurotransmitters</u>**

The balance of neurotransmitters in the brain also impacts personality characteristics.

For example, the neurotransmitter dopamine has been related with reward-seeking behaviour, and extroverts may have greater quantities of dopamine activity, pushing them to seek out social interactions and novelty. On the other hand, introverts may have greater acetylcholine activity, which is associated with focus and reflection.

## **Early Life Experiences**

While genetics and neurobiology play a crucial influence in creating personality characteristics, early life circumstances also impact an individual's introversion or extroversion. Parenting practices, early environment, and cultural influences may all contribute to the development of introverted dispositions.

For example, children reared in environments that favour quiet pondering and alone play may be more prone to demonstrate introverted tendencies.

## **Introversion as an Evolutionary Adaptation**

Some experts think that introversion may have developed as an adaptive characteristic. In ancient circumstances, introverts who were more attentive and watchful would have been more adapted to notice possible hazards or resources in their surroundings.

This heightened sensitivity and meditative temperament would have offered survival advantages in some circumstances.

## **Personality Stability and Fluidity**

It is crucial to recognize that personality characteristics, including introversion, are not static and may fluctuate over time owing to varied life events and developmental phases. While genetics and neurology provide the framework for an individual's personality, contextual influences, personal development, and adaptive actions may contribute to variances in personality characteristics.

## Cognitive Processing and Creative Potential

Introversion's specific cognitive processing style contributes to the creative potential of persons on the introverted end of the spectrum. The degree of reflection and thought that introverts engage in helps them to create distinctive ideas and seek new solutions to issues.

Introverts usually succeed at tasks that involve concentrated concentration, such as writing, drawing, and research, where they may employ their contemplative tendency to dive deep into their ideas and emotions.

## Emotional Intensity and Empathy

Introverts generally sense emotions with heightened intensity owing to their higher sensitivity to internal and external stimuli. While this may lead to times of reflection and self-discovery, it also enhances their aptitude for empathy and understanding.

Introverts may be more attentive to the emotions of others, making them compassionate listeners and useful companions. Their capacity to connect on a deeper emotional level may generate meaningful and true connections.

## Solitude as a Source of Rejuvenation

Contrary to the perception that introverts dislike social contact, seclusion is a vital source of regeneration for them. Spending time alone enables introverts to recover their energies and process their thoughts and emotions.

Solitude gives a chance for reflection, creative thought, and personal progress. Recognizing and honouring an introvert's desire for isolation may boost their general well-being and productivity.

## Managing Stress and Coping Mechanisms

The way introverts handle stress and deal with hurdles could vary from their extroverted counterparts. While extroverts may seek social support during stressful times, introverts may choose to work through their problems inside or seek comfort in solitary pastimes.

Understanding these coping methods may help introverts manage stressful circumstances more efficiently and obtain the aid they need in a manner that matches their personality.

## The Impact of Culture on Society

Cultural and cultural standards could alter the impression and acceptability of introversion. In civilizations that value friendliness, assertiveness, and gregariousness, introverted qualities may be misinterpreted or underestimated.

Creating awareness and appreciation for introversion as a positive personality attribute helps establish cultures that encourage difference and give opportunities for both introverts and extroverts to achieve.

## Balancing Introverted and Extroverted Qualities

It is crucial to highlight that introversion and extroversion are not mutually exclusive, and persons often contain elements from both sides of the spectrum.

Ambiverts, for example, display a balanced blend of introverted and extroverted qualities, adjusting their behaviour based on the circumstances. Embracing and balancing these qualities may increase an individual's social flexibility and communication ability.

## **Harnessing the Power of Introversion**

Acknowledging the qualities and benefits of introversion may enable people to leverage their particular talents to their advantage.

Creating surroundings that recognize and accept introverted tendencies may lead to improved productivity, creativity, and general well-being for both people and companies.

## **Appreciating Diversity in Personality**

Understanding the science behind introversion underlines the variety of human nature and the number of ways people interpret the world.

Rather than perceiving introversion as a restriction or fault, it is vital to welcome and respect the distinct viewpoints that introverts bring to society.

The science underlying introversion reveals crucial insights into the chemical, neurological, and genetic foundation of this key personality feature. From genetic characteristics and brain activity to emotional intensity and cognitive processing, introversion is a dynamic aspect of human personality generated by a complex combination of nature and nurture.

Embracing the special characteristics of introverts may enhance empathy, inclusivity, and a broader grasp of the many ways people see the world. Embracing introversion as a key and fundamental feature of human nature strengthens our interactions, relationships, and a collective journey toward a more compassionate and welcoming society.

# Chapter 3

## <u>THE INNER WORLD OF INTROVERTS</u>

The earth is a noisy place, full with loud, cheerful, and sociable individuals - the exuberant extroverts. Amidst them, there is the other type of the aloof and taciturn bunch, the inscrutable introverts.

Carl Jung, the Swiss psychiatrist initially popularised the notion of extroversion and introversion. No one is born an extrovert or an introvert - life's events and environmental circumstances enable any of the attributes to dominate a personality.

Extroverts get noticed and, thus, we feel the world is full with them. There are as many introverts, but they desire to stay invisible.

Extroverts have a lively disposition — outgoing, social, and responsive — and are outstanding at team play. Extroverts like team sports and take their energy from others.

They detest being alone, always seeking the companionship of family, friends, or coworkers. Extremely gregarious and sociable, it is no wonder that they are the life of each event they attend. They tend to be aggressive and thrive in fast-paced situations.

Introverts could be the exact opposites. They are peaceful folks, who appreciate their isolation and are highly comfortable with being alone. They find consolation in their inner world and would wish to calmly reflect, even introspect and think out their beliefs.

In our day of speed and innovation, being heard and seen has more relevance than being watched and appreciated. Style is selected over content, form over function and, consequently, the classic introvert with a quiet, retiring character tends to stay in obscurity in this new paradigm.

Speak when you're spoken to' is not part of the culture anymore. One needs to be an active and fluent speaker, demonstrating social skills with little or no inhibitions. In fact, extroversion is seen as a significant part in the formula for success. In other words, you may be effective but you need to be popular as well to reach the top.

## The Extrovert Myth

To produce outgoing extroverted personalities, business schools by and large adopt the case study approach putting major emphasis on effective articulation. Students who are great communicators with a quick wit and repartee have a big edge over their silent classmates, who may genuinely have superior insights and wisdom to share to the group.

The trick is how you play to your strengths. Research findings suggest that introverts demonstrate superior thinking and decision-making ability and they are able to give a relaxing impact to a frantic situation.

Advanced brain study employing F-MRIs scans reveals that introverts have an excellent supply of blood to areas in the brain that are crucial for strong memory and executive functions like thinking, planning, and so on.

In the hyper-connected world where attention spans last only seconds, maintaining focus without becoming dislocated and preserving one's equipment are two very vital skills that any business and any human group are in need of.

Introverts listen better and their sensitivity to new ideas is quite outstanding. This makes them good leaders for a team of extroverts. In a classroom atmosphere, soft-spoken team leaders who are in charge of project assignments are likely to be substantially more successful working with a set of aggressive team members.

## **Power of Introverts**

Introversion, therefore, is not a disorder; it is a personality characteristic. The ambition to become an extrovert has resulted in the establishment of a multimillion-dollar training industry and costly self-styled gurus who promise mystical therapies.

Yes, there does exist a limited number of severely introverted folks who reject any human engagement.

They may have psychological concerns and may require professional support in terms of therapy or other therapeutic procedures.

For the remainder, introversion is simply fine and does not demand any substantial modification in conduct or attitude.

## CAUSES OF INTROVERSION

Are you born introverted or is it something you grow through time? Introverts likely form owing to a mix of both nature and environment. The way that your body's physiology reacts to the outer world plays a major element in defining your amount of extroversion and introversion.

On a physiological level, a network of neurons present in the brainstem known as the reticular activating system (RAS) is responsible for controlling arousal levels including wakefulness and transitions between sleeping and waking.

The RAS also plays a function in limiting how much information you take in when you are awake. When faced with prospective threats in the environment, the RAS elevates arousal levels so you can be vigilant and ready to cope with danger.

Each individual has a baseline set point in terms of arousal level. Some individuals seem to naturally have a substantially greater set point, whilst others have a much lower set point.

These arousal levels might be conceived of as a continuum. According to his arousal hypothesis of extroversion:

15% of persons have a minimum set point, indicating they fundamentally have low arousal levels.

15% of persons have a high setpoint, suggesting they naturally tend to be more aroused.

70% of individuals lay somewhere in the centre of the spectrum.

Introverts have naturally high levels of arousal. Because of these high arousal levels, introverts prefer to seek activities and circumstances where they may escape from overstimulation. Alone time affords them the ability to study and reflect on what they have learned.

## Signs That You Are an Introvert

You may find yourself thinking, Am I an introvert? Or maybe you're wondering whether someone in your life fits into this group.

## 1. Being Around Lots of People Drains Your Energy

Do you ever feel exhausted after spending time with a lot of people? After a day of dealing with people, do you frequently need to retire to a quiet area and spend a considerable length of time with yourself?

One of the fundamental elements of this personality type is that introverts have to waste energy in social conditions, unlike extroverts who receive energy from such encounters.

That doesn't imply that introverts shun social encounters totally. Many introverts actually adore spending time among others, but they tend to prefer the company of close friends.

While an extrovert might attend a party with the objective to meet new people, an introvert expects to spend time speaking with outstanding friends.

## 2. You Enjoy Solitude

As an introvert, your notion of a good time is a tranquil day for yourself to pursue your hobbies and interests. Activities like time alone with a good book, a calm nature stroll, or watching your favourite television show make you feel revived and invigorated.

This does not imply that introverts wish to be alone all the time. Many introverts appreciate spending time with friends and communicating with recognized folks in social contexts.

The essential thing to remember is that after a full day of social engagement, an introvert will often want to escape to a quiet spot to think, reflect, and recover.

If spending a few hours alone looks like your idea of a nice time, you simply could be an introvert.

## 3. You Have a Small Group of Close Friends

One frequent misunderstanding regarding introverts is that they don't like people. While introverts typically do not like a big amount of socialising, they do adore having a limited group of friends with whom they are incredibly close.

Instead of having a broad social circle of individuals they know merely on a superficial level, introverts prefer to cling to deep, long-lasting relationships defined by a considerable degree of closeness and intimacy.

Researchers have noticed that persons strong in this attribute tend to have a smaller network of friends.

Of the several qualities of introverts, one is that they tend to build significant and important connections with people closest to them. They also like to connect with individuals on a one-on-one basis rather than in a massive group situation.

If your social circle tends to be tiny but incredibly close, there's a reasonably significant likelihood you are an introvert.

While extroverts often have a vast range of friends and acquaintances, introverts typically pick their pals significantly more carefully.

## 4. People May Find It Difficult to Get to Know You

Introverts are often considered as calm, reserved, and mellow, and are often mistaken as being bashful.

While some introverts definitely are shy, people should not misinterpret an introvert's reserve with timidity. In many cases, folks with this personality type just prefer to choose their words carefully and not spend time or energy on pointless chit-chat.

If you are the quiet kind and a little reticent, you probably are an introvert.

## 5. Too Much Stimulation Leaves You Feeling Distracted

When introverts have to spend time in activities or circumstances that are exceptionally hectic, they could wind up feeling distracted and overwhelmed.

Extroverts, on the other hand, prefer to flourish in circumstances where there is a lot of action and little possibility of becoming bored.

Researchers have found that introverts tend to be more readily distracted than extroverts,5 which is part of the reason why introverts tend to prefer a calmer, less hectic atmosphere. If you tend to feel overwhelmed in chaotic social environments, you may be an introvert.

## 6. You Are Very Self-Aware

Because introverts tend to be inward-turning, they also spend a great lot of time researching their own interior experiences. If you feel that you have a good grasp and insight into yourself, your motives, and your emotions, you could be more of an introvert.

Introverts tend to appreciate thinking about and dissecting things in their own heads. Self-awareness and self-understanding are crucial to introverts, hence they often commit a great lot of effort to learning more about oneself.

If you believe that you are self-aware and adore gaining profound information about yourself, then you could be more of an introvert.

Self-awareness is one of the numerous attributes of introverts. They prefer to pursue things they like, wonder about their lives, and read literature that examine subjects and issues that are significant to them.

## 7. You Like to Learn by Watching

Where extroverts tend to desire to get right in and learn by hands-on experience, introverts frequently prefer learning by observation. Extroverts learn by trial and error, whereas introverts prefer to observe before trying anything new.

Introverts like to see others do a work, often repeatedly, until they believe that they can reproduce the actions on their own. When introverts do learn from personal experience, they prefer to practise someplace alone where they may build their skills and talents without having to perform for an audience.

If you tend to learn more by observing rather than doing, there is a likelihood that you have a more introverted personality.

## 8. You Are Drawn to Jobs That Involve Independence

As you may assume, jobs that need a great degree of social contact usually hold little interest to those strong in introversion.

On the other hand, careers that include working autonomously are often a fantastic option for introverts. For example, an introvert could appreciate working as a writer, accountant, computer programmer, graphic designer, pharmacist, or artist.

## Introversion vs. Shyness

It is vital to note that introversion does not always correspond to shyness. In The Development of Shyness and Social Withdrawal, Louis Schmidt and Arnold Buss explain, "Sociability refers to the motive, strong or weak, of wanting to be with others, whereas shyness refers to behaviour when with others, inhibited or uninhibited, as well as feelings of tension and discomfort."

Shyness demonstrates a dread of people or social conditions. Introverts, on the other hand, just prefer not to spend amounts of time socialising with other individuals.

Introverts do love being with folks with whom they are close. They find partaking in "small talk" annoying but do adore having deep, meaningful talks. Introverts also prefer to contemplate before speaking.

They seek to have a thorough knowledge of a topic before they express an opinion or attempt to give an explanation.

### **Introversion vs. Depression**

If you find yourself asking, Am I an introvert or depressed? It's crucial to remember that anybody may feel sadness, whether they are an introvert or extrovert.

If you are retiring from social engagements or activities to the point where you are feeling sad, apprehensive, melancholy, or concerned, this may be a symptom of depression—regardless of your personality type.

Some research demonstrates that introversion may raise the probability of getting loneliness, depression, and anxiety. If you are suffering these or any other mental health difficulties, be sure to speak to a doctor or mental health expert.

Similarly, if you're questioning, Am I an introvert or antisocial? Chatting to a mental health expert may help you find an answer. The major distinction between being an introvert and being antisocial is that introverts are socially involved (in a manner that appears comfortable to them) and those who are antisocial choose not to be.

People who are antisocial frequently find it tough to live in a culture where they are expected to have even minimum social contact or behave in a socially acceptable manner. If you're suffering from this, talking to a mental health specialist may also help you discover whether your antisocial conduct is associated with a related mental health problem.

### **How Introverts Process Information**

Introverts and extroverts have various techniques of connecting with the world around them, including how they absorb information. Understanding how introverts consume information is crucial for respecting their specific cognitive style and the attributes they offer to varied contexts.

### **1.	Internal	Reflection	and Introspection:**

Introverts tend to process information by inward thinking and introspection. They typically want to take the time to think deeply about a subject before reacting or forming conclusions.

This thoughtful strategy helps introverts to analyse content from diverse views and explore its repercussions carefully.

## 2.    Thoughtful    Listening    and Observation:

When involved in lectures or group debates, introverts are more prone to be attentive listeners and observers. They may carefully note verbal and nonverbal signs, which helps them appreciate the nuances of the discussion and the emotions underpinning the relationship.

## 3. Depth over Breadth:

Unlike extroverts, who may thrive on a vast variety of social contacts and stimuli, introverts prefer depth over breadth when assimilating information. They are more interested in researching thoroughly into a specific topic or notion rather than fast examining multiple areas. This quest for depth helps introverts to obtain a full knowledge of the subjects that attract their attention.

## 4. Internalising before Externalizing:

Introverts often absorb knowledge before externalising their thoughts or ideas. They may take time digesting information internally, studying it from numerous viewpoints, and forming their replies before expressing it orally. As a consequence, introverts may look quieter in social circumstances, taking more time to respond to disputes.

## 5. Need for Solitude:

Solitude is crucial for introverts while digesting information. They need calm and uninterrupted time alone to dwell over their ideas, think on events, and refill their mental resources. Solitude helps introverts to process information without external interruptions and offers them room for deeper reflection.

## 6. Preparing in Advance:

Introverts typically like to prepare in advance for social meetings or events where information processing is crucial. They may anticipate potential conversations or presentations, gather knowledge, and arrange their views ahead to feel more confident and comfortable during the real engagement.

## 7. Focusing on Key Details:

In information processing, introverts prefer to concentrate on key details and relevant information. They may be less interested in superficial or inconsequential details of a subject and instead focus on learning the key ideas and fundamental principles.

## 8. Empathy and Emotional Sensitivity:

Introverts' information processing is frequently braided with their empathy and emotional sensitivity. They are sensitive to the sentiments and opinions of others, which helps them to grasp difficult interpersonal dynamics and sympathise with other viewpoints.

## 9. Integrating Past Experiences:

Introverts prefer to incorporate earlier experiences into their present information processing. They use their previous knowledge and lessons learnt to make connections and generate meaning from new information.

## 10. Openness to New Ideas:

Despite their penchant for depth, introverts could be receptive to discovering new ideas and opinions. They may explore unknown content with curiosity and receptiveness if it matches with their interests and views.

How introverts perceive information is defined by introspective contemplation, meticulous listening, and a preference for depth over breadth. They thrive alone, where they may plunge deeply into their thoughts and ideas. Introverts are thoughtful and contemplative folks who assimilate knowledge before presenting their opinions freely.

Their empathetic character, emotional sensitivity, and integration of earlier experiences lead to their particular style of thinking and interacting with the world.

By identifying and accepting the cognitive style of introverts, we may establish better communication, create inclusive settings, and harness the strengths that introverts give to different scenarios.

Embracing the multiplicity of information processing ways strengthens our connections and develops a more caring and understanding community.

# Chapter 4

## <u>CRAZY MISCONCEPTIONS ABOUT INTROVERTS</u>

Introverts have long been the object of innumerable misunderstandings and stereotypes, resulting in a variety of bizarre and erroneous opinions about their personality features and actions.

These views generally miss the true nature of introversion and could foster misunderstandings and prejudices. In this extensive analysis, we refute some of the most prevalent and outrageous assumptions about introverts, throwing light on the reality behind their distinguishing qualities.

### 1. Introverts are Shy and Socially Awkward:

One of the most frequent stereotypes about introverts is that they are timid and socially uncomfortable. While some introverts may demonstrate shyness in particular settings, introversion itself is not connected with social anxiety. Introverts may feel more comfortable in quieter or more personal social circumstances, but they may participate in social interactions with ease and confidence provided their requirements are addressed.

## 2. Introverts Hate People and Are Antisocial:

Another stupid assumption is that introverts despise people and want to be alone all the time. This couldn't be farther from the truth. Introverts adore meaningful connections and deep relationships, yet they may crave more isolation to restore their energies after social events. Introverts may be gregarious, charming, and like socialising; they just need to balance their social contacts with times of isolation.

## 3. Introverts Are Boring and Uninteresting:

Some misunderstandings portray introverts as boring and uninteresting folks who lack enthusiasm in their life. On the contrary, introverts often have rich inner worlds, profound interests, and creative hobbies that may not always be visible on the surface. Their introspective tendency may lead to unique thoughts and thought-provoking conversations.

## 4. Introverts Are Not Team Players:

It's a myth that introverts are not team players or do not contribute successfully in group circumstances. Introverts give crucial attributes to cooperation, such as attentive listening, methodical thinking, and the capacity to manage disagreements. They may not dominate group interactions, but their opinions and contributions may be vital to the team's success.

## 5. Introverts Dislike Public Speaking:

While public speaking could be nerve-wracking for certain people, it is not a universal fact for all introverts. Introverts may feel more comfortable and confident while speaking in front of an audience, particularly when they are well-prepared and excited about the issue. Public speaking preferences vary widely among introverts, just as they do among extroverts.

## 6. Introverts Are Emotionally Repressed:

Contrary to the idea that introverts conceal their emotions, many introverts have rich emotional lives and communicate their feelings in meaningful ways. Their introspective tendency helps individuals to absorb feelings inside before expressing them with others, resulting in more profound and authentic expressions of emotion.

## 7. Introverts Don't Have Leadership Skills:

Another popular misunderstanding is that introverts lack leadership talents or are not fit for leadership roles. In truth, introverts may be fantastic leaders. They frequently demonstrate traits such as active listening, empathy, and a capacity to develop inclusive workplaces that inspire and drive their colleagues.

## 8. Introverts Are Not Adventurous:

The impression that introverts are not adventurous or open to experiencing new things is far from the truth. Introverts may approach unfamiliar circumstances with caution, but they are not opposed to exploring the world and enjoying uncommon encounters. Introverts could find enjoyment in calm retreats, cerebral interests, and alone exploration.

## 9. Introverts Can't Be Successful in Social Jobs:

Some misunderstandings indicate that introverts cannot flourish in vocations that need regular social contact. However, many brilliant introverts thrive in social vocations such as counselling, teaching, sales, and leadership. Their capacity to empathise, listen closely, and communicate on a deeper level could be advantageous in certain situations.

## 10. Introverts Lack Confidence:

It is crucial to discern between introversion and lack of confidence. Introverts may take time to ponder and organise their views before speaking, which could be misunderstood as a lack of confidence. In truth, introverts may be self-assured and forceful, particularly when discussing things they are passionate about.

## 11. Introverts Are Unassertive and Passive:

It is a fallacy that introverts are inert and unable to exert themselves. While they may not be as blatantly strong as extroverts, introverts often communicate their opinions and desires effectively and assertively when given the chance.

Their attitude to assertiveness may vary from that of extroverts, since they may prefer to address difficulties by serious thinking and private talks.

## 12. Introverts Are Always Serious and Lacking a Sense of Humor:

Some stereotypes depict introverts as serious and humourless persons. However, introverts have a specific sense of humour that may be more subtle and nuanced. They prefer wit, sophisticated wordplay, and comedy that engages their mind. While they may not always be the light of the party, introverts may surprise others with their wit and rare bursts of comedy.

## 13. Introverts Are Unfriendly and Cold:

Introverts are usually incorrectly seen as disagreeable or chilly because of their guarded approach. In truth, introverts may develop powerful and durable bonds. They may take longer to open up and develop trust, but once they feel comfortable, introverts may be warm, devoted, and loving companions.

## 14. Introverts Don't Enjoy Going Out:

Another fallacy is that introverts avoid going out and engaging in social gatherings totally. While introverts may choose calmer situations, they nevertheless adore communicating on their own. They like meaningful chats and favour quality over quantity when it comes to social connections.

**15. Introverts Can't Be Spontaneous:**
Some people assume that introverts are excessively strict and unable to welcome spontaneity. However, introverts could be receptive to unplanned interactions when they align with their interests and views. They may want some degree of preparation to prevent overwhelming circumstances, but they may also appreciate unexpected activities that relate with their interests.

**16. Introverts Don't Need Social Interaction:**
While introverts love their alone time, they also want social involvement and human connection. Like everyone else, introverts gain from pleasant social experiences that produce emotional well-being and a feeling of belonging. They may just seek a balance between social participation and isolation.

## 17. Introverts Lack Confidence in Public Speaking:

A frequent misunderstanding about introverts is that they lack confidence in public speaking or perform badly in public circumstances.

However, many introverts are good and confident public presenters, especially when they are knowledgeable and enthusiastic about the topic matter. They may approach public speaking in a particular manner, such as well-prepared and deliberate speeches.

## 18. Introverts Are Easily Bored:

Some beliefs claim that introverts grow bored fast or fail to find satisfaction in different pursuits. On the contrary, introverts typically indulge in hobbies and pastimes that catch their thoughts and allow for intensive concentration. They may select meaningful and intellectually stimulating activities over frequent external stimuli.

## 19. Introverts Are Not Team Players:

While introverts may prefer alone work at times, they may still be outstanding team contributors. They bring their own viewpoints, give meaningful ideas, and stimulate cooperation within the team. Introverts may flourish in occupations that enable them to contribute profoundly and meaningfully to the team's aims.

## 20. Introverts Can't Be Outgoing:

The belief that introverts cannot be social or express joy is a mistake. Introverts may be talkative, outspoken, and passionate, particularly in environments that relate with their hobbies or passions. Their external representation of joy may be more subtle, yet it does not decrease their actual emotion.

Correcting these ridiculous misunderstandings about introverts is crucial for establishing a more accurate and empathetic awareness of their personality features and activities. Introverts are not characterised by stereotypes or constraints but are persons with distinct strengths, interests, and contributions to society.

Embracing the genuine nature of introverts may lead to more inclusive cultures, enhanced communication, and healthier interpersonal interactions that appreciate the different viewpoints of both introverts and extroverts equally. Ultimately, appreciating the variety and diversity of human personality enriches our connections, empathy, and appreciation for the beauty of uniqueness.

# Chapter 5

## <u>THRIVING AS AN INTROVERT</u>

Being an introvert comes with its own set of different issues in a culture that typically encourages extroverted qualities. However, introverts possess several skills and talents that assist them to overcome these obstacles and flourish in other sectors of life.

In this lengthy investigation, we look into the tactics and approaches introverts may apply to confront problems, accept their real selves, and succeed in both personal and professional settings.

**1. Embracing Self-Acceptance:**
The first step in handling problems as an introvert is adopting self-acceptance. Recognizing and accepting one's introverted nature as a true and valuable component of

their personality is crucial for acquiring confidence and resilience.

Instead of seeking to adapt to extroverted standards, introverts should showcase their virtues, such as their reflection, empathy, and analytical approach to problem-solving.

## 2. Honouring the Need for Solitude:

Introverts require ample time alone to recharge their mental resources and process information.

Conquering the challenge of feeling exhausted or overwhelmed in social circumstances necessitates setting apart defined moments of isolation for introspection and self-renewal.

Prioritising alone time aids introverts to bear the hardships of regular life with more serenity.

**3. Finding Empowering Social Spaces:**
While introverts may not adore enormous, crowded gatherings, they may uncover powerful social spaces that suit their inclinations. Choosing smaller, more personal events or one-on-one chats may promote meaningful relationships without exhausting introverts with excessive stimulus. Seeking out like-minded folks who respect and understand introversion develops fruitful connections.

**4. Developing Effective Communication Skills:**
Conquering the challenge of expressing yourself in social contexts includes acquiring strong communication skills. Introverts may employ active listening, meaningful replies, and powerful communication to convey their thoughts and feelings effectively.

By valuing their contributions in group talks and offering ideas with confidence, introverts may make their voices heard.

## 5. Leveraging Introverted Strengths in the Workplace:

In the business sphere, introverts may address challenges by using their specific strengths. Their careful analysis, attention to detail, and ability to work independently make them ideal team members. Emphasising their problem-solving aptitude and listening skills may lead to recognition and success in the field.

## 6. Pushing Comfort Zones Gradually:

Conquering hurdles as an introvert entails steadily stretching comfort zones in a controlled and sustainable way. Engaging in social settings that fit with personal interests and objectives may help introverts enhance their confidence and minimise anxiety.

By taking modest steps beyond their comfort zones, introverts may increase their social horizons without feeling overwhelmed.

## 7. Developing Emotional Intelligence:

Emotional intelligence plays a key element in mastering challenges as an introvert. Understanding and managing emotions, both in oneself and in others, improves interpersonal relationships and develops a better feeling of connection.

Emotional intelligence helps introverts to manage social dynamics more successfully and react empathetically to different conditions.

## 8. Setting Boundaries:

Conquering the challenge of feeling emotionally exhausted or overstimulated includes establishing suitable limits. Introverts should convey their need for alone time and space to recharge to their friends, family, and workplace. By defining clear limitations and advocating for their well-being, introverts may avoid burnout and maintain a decent work-life balance.

## 9. Cultivating Networking Strategies:

Networking is an essential component of personal and professional growth. Introverts may address networking challenges by adopting techniques that correlate with their talents.

This may involve locating smaller networking events, organising in advance, and focussing on creating meaningful relationships with a few persons rather than attempting to network with a vast number of people.

## 10. Celebrating Personal Achievements:

Finally, tackling challenges as an introvert includes acknowledging personal successes, no matter how minor they may appear.

Recognizing and valuing achievement, growth, and venturing out of comfort zones improves high self-esteem and stimulates future personal development.

## 11. Leveraging Technology and Online Platforms:

In an increasingly digital environment, introverts may overcome challenges by embracing technology and online platforms to engage with people.

Virtual networking events, social media, and online organisations provide introverts the ability to make contacts at their own speed and in a less frightening context. The skill to participate in writing communication may also be advantageous for introverts since it provides them time to carefully organise their responses.

## 12. Seeking Support and Understanding:

Conquering problems as an introvert entails getting aid from understanding friends, family, and coworkers. Surrounding oneself with others who realise and respect their introverted disposition may produce a positive and supportive atmosphere.

Having individuals who respect the need for solitude and the necessity of meaningful discussion fosters a sense of belonging and decreases feelings of loneliness.

## 13. Challenging Stereotypes and Educating Others:

Introverts may take an active part in fixing problems by overcoming assumptions and informing people about the spectrum of personality types.

By sharing their experiences and opinions, introverts may enhance awareness and develop a more inclusive understanding of introversion. Open talks and fruitful encounters may lead to better understanding and respect for the particular traits that introverts bring to the table.

## 14. Engaging in Personal Development:

Conquering challenges takes ongoing personal progress. Introverts could participate in activities such as reading, attending seminars, or enrolling in public speaking lessons to strengthen their communication and social skills.

Developing a growth mentality and a readiness to learn and adapt may assist introverts to manage different conditions with more comfort and confidence.

## 15. Celebrating Introverted Role Models:

Recognizing and appreciating successful introverted role models may be motivating and affirming for introverts. By recognizing excellent people who embrace and prosper as introverts, they may disprove limiting preconceptions and recognize that success comes in various forms and personalities.

Identifying with introverted role models may enhance self-esteem and motivate introverts to pursue their ambitions boldly.

## 16. Embracing the Power of Introverted Creativity:

Many introverts enjoy a rich inner world of creativity and imagination. Embracing and using this inventiveness may be a terrific technique to address issues.

Engaging in creative undertakings, whether by writing, painting, music, or other hobbies, encourages introverts to express themselves truly and share their distinct ideas with the world.

## 17. Embracing Gratitude and Mindfulness:

Cultivating a practice of appreciation and mindfulness may greatly benefit introverts in confronting issues. By emphasising on the good characteristics of their introverted nature and being present at the moment, introverts may develop resilience and nurture a feeling of tranquillity among life's challenges.

## 18. Recognizing the Value of Introverted Leadership:

Introverts may surpass issues associated with leadership by understanding and embracing their own leadership style. They may lead with empathy, active listening, and savvy decision-making.

Appreciating the value of introverted leadership may inspire introverts to pursue leadership positions confidently and make a good influence in their communities and companies.

Tackling problems as an introvert entails recognizing self-acceptance, leveraging strengths, and obtaining aid from understanding others. Utilising technology, questioning prejudices, and investing in personal growth are key approaches for overcoming social and professional difficulties.

By respecting personal triumphs and embracing introverted creativity, introverts may traverse life with confidence and honesty. Embracing gratitude, mindfulness, and introverted leadership further allows introverts to prosper in a culture that appreciates their particular talents.

With perseverance, self-awareness, and a willingness to learn, introverts may transcend challenges, develop meaningful relationships, and have a good influence on themselves and the people around them.

# Chapter 6

## <u>PARENTING AN INTROVERT</u>

Parenting is a journey filled with delights, sorrows, and the discovery of each child's unique individuality. For parents of introverted children, identifying and supporting their child's needs and skills is crucial for fostering a healthy and supportive culture.

In this inquiry, we go into the subtleties of parenting an introvert, giving insights, suggestions, and ways to support their child's well-being, progress, and self-acceptance.

### 1. Embrace and Accept Introversion:
The first step in parenting an introvert is to embrace and respect their child's introverted disposition. Recognizing that introversion is a true and important

personality feature is vital for developing a loving and supportive culture.

Parents should avoid encouraging their kids to become more extroverted and instead celebrate their special skills, such as their intellect, sensitivity, and creativity.

## 2. Create a Safe and Calm Home Environment:

Introverted youngsters typically flourish in calm and tranquil surroundings. Providing a tranquil home atmosphere allows introverted children to regain their mental energy and indulge in contemplation without feeling overwhelmed.

Creating designated spaces for alone time or quiet hobbies may help introverted adolescents feel protected and encouraged.

## 3. Respect the Need for Solitude:

Respecting the desire for isolation is vital when raising an introverted kid. Introverts renew their energy via alone time and reflection, hence it is crucial to allow them the space and time they require.

Parents should avoid overloading introverted youngsters with regular social obligations and instead enable them to schedule alone time to recoup.

**4. Encourage Open Communication:**
Open communication is crucial in interpreting an introverted child's ideas, emotions, and experiences.

Parents should build an environment of trust and encourage their kids to communicate their concerns and fears freely. Active listening and confirming their child's emotions display support and establish a strong parent-child relationship.

## 5. Foster Empathy and Emotional Intelligence:

Introverted children usually demonstrate heightened emotional intelligence and sensitivity. Parents may further foster these qualities by exhibiting empathy, addressing emotions freely, and encouraging their kids to understand and express their feelings constructively.

This emotional awareness assists introverted teenagers to navigate social situations with sensitivity and compassion.

## 6. Provide Opportunities for Thoughtful Exploration:

Introverted teenagers tend to enjoy careful investigation and creative pastimes. Parents may give possibilities for their kids to participate in activities that stimulate their hobbies and creativity, such as reading, writing, painting, or other sorts of creative expression. These hobbies could boost their self-esteem and feeling of contentment.

**7. Encourage Meaningful Social Connections:**

While introverted children may not crave regular social contact, they nonetheless benefit from meaningful relationships with others.

Parents might encourage their kids to build close ties with like-minded others who understand and respect their introverted disposition. Quality over quantity in social contact is crucial for introverted adolescents to feel understood and supported.

**8. Advocate for Their Needs in School and Extracurriculars:**

Advocating for their child's needs in school and extracurricular activities is crucial for parenting an introvert. Parents should engage with instructors and coaches about their child's introversion and discuss ways for adapting their learning and social preferences. Providing flexibility and understanding may assist their child's academic and personal success.

## 9. Teach Assertive Communication Skills:

Introverted youngsters may face trouble in expressing themselves assertively in social circumstances.

Parents may support their kids develop assertive communication skills, such as expressing their views and opinions forcefully, creating limits, and advocating for their needs. These qualities assist introverted children to manage social circumstances with confidence.

## 10. Celebrate Their Achievements and Growth:

Celebrating their child's triumphs, whether major or tiny, develops excellent self-esteem and self-acceptance. Parents should acknowledge and encourage their child's efforts, noting that introverted kids may display their strengths in more subtle ways.

Celebrating development and achievement in different facets of their child's life encourages them to accept their genuine self.

## 11. Encourage Balanced Social Engagement:

While introverted children may appreciate spending time alone, it is vital to develop healthy social interaction. Parents may assist their kids discover a good middle ground between solitude and social contact. Rather than pressing them to attend many social events, parents should cooperate with their kids to pick a few important gatherings or activities that coincide with their interests.

## 12. Provide Opportunities for Reflection and Journaling:

Introverted youngsters often gain from opportunities for introspection and writing. Encouraging children to maintain a notepad or diary allows them to process their ideas and feelings quietly. Writing may be a therapeutic outlet for introverted adolescents to evaluate their feelings and get insights into their experiences.

## 13. Support Introverted Leadership Qualities:

Parenting an introverted youngster includes discovering and nurturing their leadership talents. Introverts usually succeed in leadership settings thanks to their methodical decision-making, sensitivity, and capacity to listen to others' viewpoints. Encouraging their youngsters to take leadership positions encourages them to make a constructive effect on their neighbourhood and beyond.

## 14. Teach Social Skills in a Comfortable Setting:

While introverted children may feel nervous at huge social occasions, parents may teach them social skills in a safe and low-pressure environment. Playdates with close friends or family members help introverted youngsters to practise social interactions at their own tempo, gradually gaining confidence and comfort in social contexts.

## 15. Set Realistic Expectations:

Parenting an introverted kid includes creating appropriate expectations and acknowledging their own triumphs. Introverts may not always conform with the extroverted criteria, and that is absolutely OK. Rather of comparing them to more extroverted acquaintances, parents should praise and congratulate their child's achievements based on their specific skills and talents.

## 16. Cultivate Mindfulness and Coping Strategies:

Helping introverted youngsters gain mindfulness and coping techniques is vital for controlling stress and anxiety. Parents might provide relaxation methods, mindfulness activities, or breathing exercises to support emotional well-being. Teaching introverted children how to deal with stressful circumstances could equip them to tackle issues with fortitude.

## 17. Provide Opportunities for Independent Learning:

Introverted youngsters often prosper in solitary learning situations. Parents may foster this aspect of their child's development by allowing opportunity for self-directed learning and discovery.

Reading books, partaking in hobbies, or pursuing interests outside of formal schooling may boost their intellectual curiosity and desire for learning.

## 18. Emphasise Personal Growth Over Social Comparison:

Parenting an introverted kid entails pushing personal development and self-improvement above cultural comparison. Comparing shy youngsters to more outgoing friends could lead to feelings of inferiority. Instead, parents should encourage their kids to develop specific objectives and celebrate their accomplishments on their particular route.

Parenting an introverted kid requires appreciating their distinctive qualities, respecting their need for seclusion, and giving opportunity for personal development and social interaction.

Encouraging open communication, encouraging their interests, and building emotional intelligence produce a pleasant and helpful parent-child interaction. As parents develop their introverted child's strengths and help them to handle social situations with confidence, introverted children may grow into self-assured and honest people who make essential contributions to the world around them.

By fostering a caring and understanding atmosphere, parents may assist their introverted children grow and bloom as they begin on a pleasant life path.